Special thanks for the use of photo by
Evgenit@pixabay.com

While every precaution has been taken in the preparation of this book, the publisher assumes no responsibility for errors or omissions, or for damages resulting from the use of the information contained herein.

HEART OF A WOODEN DOLL

First edition. August 6, 2023.

Copyright © 2023 Barbara McDannell.

ISBN: 979-8223514404

Written by Barbara McDannell.

Table of Contents

This book if first and foremost dedicated to my best friend, Michael Scott Ferguson. We met when we were five and spent the last fifty five years growing together and celebrating each other.

My "twin" brother John who first helped compile these poems into a collection that could be organized and printed.

Cannot forget my other best friend, Denise, who has walked next to me through much of this healing and cheered me on every step.

Most importantly to my Savior who authored the healing of this Wooden Doll's heart

The author of this book wrote these poems during the course of healing. Her sole purpose in publishing this book is to help someone else, even if it is one person. She is a survivor of horrific sexual abuse and was trafficked by her father, his friends, and some influential leaders of the community. She lived silently and wants everyone to know that they have a voice and do not have to keep the secrets. There is hope. If this book helps even one person, the author's goal will have been reached.

The title of this book came from the first poem that I wrote on my healing journey. The poem is called the wooden doll and in that poem I talk of how I survived the horrific abuse by pretending to be a wooden doll with no face and no heart. One day, I finally realized the wooden doll did have a heart and a face and it was me. It was on that day that I realized I no longer was in danger and no longer had to keep their secrets. Once I realized there was hope, my life changed. I am only willing to publish these very personal poems so that perhaps one person can be changed and saved. Believe me, I am a miracle. I want to help. It is my greatest desire that in these words will be found courage and the ability to help someone.

Thank you,

Barbara E. McDannell

"Warning"

There is Evil in this world, it is real!
The main author and editor wish that this book will reach those
in need, thru the help of doctors, counselors, social workers,
family members and friends.
This book is not intended for little children. This set of poems is
mainly a true-life experience set in this format for artistic
purposes and written to help the many victims of abuse
overcome their pain.
It's the Authors' hope that the persons who read this book of
poems will discover the message that you are not alone and that
there is hope. Realistically there is no timeframe for someone to
overcome the pain of any kind of abuse. In real terms as long as
you believe that you a victim the abuser wins. The author wants
you to be a survivor not a victim. Release the control that the
abuser has over you, and if possible, forgive, for ultimately God
is the Judge.

Why Confide

Why would I choose in you to confide
You prefer I stay away and just hide
I have tried at times to show my face
But you refuse to allow me into your reality space
I have lived life and possess a story to tell
Things I have seen that came straight from hell
You believe that no others can really see
I belong though you deny you are a part of me
You smile and wave thinking no one knows the lie
How you stood by and let my soul slowly die
Who is that long ago, let my fate be sealed
The one who still believes I can be healed
I started way down where love no longer reaches
Life has caused me to be broken in many pieces
You are so afraid to know why I am mad
You pretend I am responsible for what's bad
So why would I choose in you to confide
The separation between us has gotten far too wide
I for now stay by no one really seen
Where I have been locked since being a teen
You refuse to allow me a way out
The pain I hold in, you seem to doubt
Go ahead and continue to pretend I don't exist

Inside of you I will continue to pound a fist
Why would I choose in you to confide
When you prefer to pretend and ask me to hide

A Child Lost

I came into this world a child pure
Thought I would be safe and secure
I was innocent and so clean
I did not know people were mean
I cried only when hungry or wet
Every need I thought would be met
I seemed to be a clean little slate
To what would become I could not wait
A fresh bright start I would think
But all of that changed in one quick blink
Suddenly I became a child lost
No one ever thought to count my cost
The first time one of them touched me
The innocent child ceased to be
I had just received a childhood lost
Forever in a world that was storm tossed
That child still loves somewhere inside deep
She is waiting for someone to hear her weep
Someone finally said the stories should be told
Someone safe who believed that she was sold
I do not think she can ever be the same
There are so many people that carry the blame
Am I forever to be a child lost

A child lied to and double crossed

UNTITILED

Abandonment
Don't let him live in your
Head for free rent
All these new words
I did not even know
How much my vision has been blurred
Memories long hidden away
Inside deep where no one knew
Now refuse in the dark to stay
Sometimes it scares me
At all this locked up inside
Making me think I am crazy
Now a safe haven found
For all the stories have
Been given a voice and sound
Still the fear you won't last
That you will leave before
This storm has really past
I am trying so hard to learn
To relax not worry but trust
My life a different way to turn
Someday a different view
I will be able to see

My life transformed and new

The Hole

There's a hole
In my soul
It is so deep
It makes me weep
No one else can see
Inside to the real me
The me I hide
Stays safe closed inside
No one knows
How deep it goes
The great big hole
Deep inside of my soul

The Well

Deep inside me there's a well
Full of stories yet to tell
Its the storehouse of all pain
The way that I learned to maintain
In not sure what still is there
Waiting for the time to share
At times I am allowed a glimpse to see
The real person that I am meant to be
My life's been viewed by jaded eyes
A life that has been based on living lies
Slowly now it is all coming out
Even though i still have my doubt
God prepared me to walk this road
He knew I would bear a heavy load
This has been a long slow life walk
It requires some time to be able to talk
My soul needs a cleansing bath
I just have to find the right path
This will help the wooden doll become real
And the well of pain a way to finally heal

I BELIEVED

Daddy said I was just a cheap useless whore
And no matter what, would never be any more
Those words hurt and reached to my very core
I didn't believe for me there was any thing different in store
They saw me as a child they could throw away
Just a big unfeeling lump of useless dried up clay
I was an object used by them to have their own way
They knew I was much too frightened to disobey
I was just one of many children they had
We all learned very quickly what things made them mad
Each of us brainwashed to believe we were the bad
Each of us thought we were alone and we were all sad
For me there was no other way of life
I was made to play the evil men's wife
I wished just once for the final cut of the knife
My misery with the blood to wash away the strife
I did not understand that they would to me lie
I believed if I told anyone I would surely die
They said there would be no time to say good bye
They said when I was gone no one would ask why
From the very day that I was on this earth born
My soul had already been battered and torn
Secrecy at all cost from me was sworn

As they used me to make their perverted porn
I have always believed that it became my sin
That perhaps it was my choice to be in
It never occurred to me I was never going to win
These games played with me starting with my own kin
Daddy said it would not matter to them if I were dead
He said they could make my blood flow bright red
I didn't trust the men I was made to lie with in bed
But they taught me to trust when I laid and bled

Questions

What if I truly am to blame
If what happened is my sin
Will I forever carry the shame
Is there reason to keep it all in
So many questions there are to ask
But I am not sure I have the right
Maybe I should just keep on the mask
Never let anyone see my true light
A little girl so scared and small
Who does she have? Where can she go?
From the depth of her soul is a call
Please show me, am I my own foe
Is there really a way to survive
To find a way through to the other side
Is that little girl still alive
Or has the real me already died

A Long Journey

I have been walking this journey for a very long time
Trying to figure out life's reason and its rhyme
It has truly been a long season in my life
A season filled with heartache and so much strife
Most of the time I have felt like I am lost
By the storms of my life blown about and tossed
It has been so hard , my Heavenly Father's voice to hear
When I am enveloped in this huge dark cloud of fear
How was I able to wander from Him so far away
It happened one step at a time...day by day
I am ready to no longer continue alone to roam
Please help me find a place I know is my home
Come gently beside me and simply take my hand
Giving me the strength and courage I need to stand

BATTERED HEART

I have a life full of memory
Not many people given the chance to see
I hold them stuffed so deep inside
Most people not allowed to see what I hide
I have a heart that has been bruised and battered
A little girls soul that was over and over shattered
I have wandered through the years just surviving life
I managed to make it despite all of the strife
I know that now I have a chance at different
It can change the way all these years have been spent
The feelings are meant to be challenged and fought
So a light to my dark world can be brought
I have a heart that's been bruised and battered
As a little girl my soul was broken and shattered
I know that today I must find a new way
Locked in this pain and grief not willing to stay
There is a future for me if I can look
A trade for all that my father took
It can be so new and so bright
It will truly change my whole world sight

THE GUN STORY

In two different rooms they slept at night
Only in their dreams were their lives alright
Three young children all soundly asleep
Until Daddy got home and up the stairs did creep
The children had no idea what was to come
But at the sound of his voice they went numb
He stood over each one until they began to awake
They had no idea of what the night would take
Down the stairs he forced the children three
My two little brothers, John, Terry, and me
The gun in his hand shown with a glint
Not one of the children had even a hint
He first held the gun up to his own head
Then announced that tonight one would be dead
He told of how these three made him so mad
How each of these children were horribly bad
The three stood together trembling with fear
So scared they were unable to shed even one tear
They huddled close to each other yet felt very alone
As they tried to survive with a plan of their own
He laughed as he held the gun to his head
The children thought he soon would be dead
That was their wish and even their prayer

They stood without moving they knew they did not dare
How could this possibly come to an end
How would the children's souls ever mend
The gun was finally set down on the table
The whole affair became a forgotten family fable
The three small children all stood in pure awe
They could not believe all they just saw
They were sent back upstairs to get into bed
The events of the night still fresh in their head
They slept all together in one bed that night
They were never able to turn off the bedroom light
All through the night not one of them slept
They just held each other and silently wept
It was never discussed among them after that day
Each child in their own time had a price they would pay
The memory of it all made the children's blood run cold
Never could that nights terror be accurately told

Who's that in the mirror

This girl looking at me from the mirror
She cannot really be me
This girl is strange and different
She knows things that could not be
The face that is reflected there
That girl there does she feel
Does she go places I do not
Is that girl or me who is real
Is there hope that we will ever be one
Each loving and knowing all there is
Becoming able to live and learn together
Taking all the power that once was his
Someday that girl looking in the mirror
I'll be proud to say that she is really me
A woman who has truly become
Someone who I am proud to be

MEMORIES

There are so many secrets that deep down reside
They have stayed there for so long inside
Now it seems as though I cannot continue to hide
With all of this I must learn to abide
There are different parts that have served me well
But they are no longer content inside to dwell
The emotions are beginning like a wave to swell
There are moments when it feels like I am in hell
How did I survive all of those many years
How did I handle all of those terrible fears
Now it feels like my insides are being poked with spears
I cannot seem to stop my eyes from producing tears
It has been obvious to me that there are still stories untold
I am not sure how long I can make them hold
With each passing date the memories are more bold
Memories of a little girl's soul unwillingly sold

A Brown Bag Story

I came to the Lord as an old brown bag
My life was like a filthy sin covered rag
He saw me without all that sin
He saw me as a beautiful valuable tin
I brought Him all that I had
A life that was sorry and sad
A life without anything left to give
A life without any reason left to live
Just an old beat up dirty brown bag
A life that was nothing but a sin soiled rag
Suddenly I heard God softly call my name
Who knew that I would never be the same
He asked me if I really wanted to change
A new container for the old to exchange
The answer was a simple yes Lord yes
You can have my life, you can take this mess
Now God has done a complete miracle
He has made my life so good and full
People say I've changed, that I am different.
It is all because to the Lord I went
God says you can bring your old brown bag
Your life's sin soaked dirty rag
He sees you void of all that sin

To Him you are a beautiful new tin
Listen as He gently quietly calls your name
Answer Him and it never has to be the same

The Untold Fairy Tale

Once upon a time lived a frightened princess
Her world and her life clouded in such a mess
An evil king ruled in the strange land
Where his every whim was a stern demand
The princess lived every day in pure dread
Never knowing when she would be summoned to his bed
The king had other men whom she could not beat
It was her job to perform and give them a treat
The king looked on as the men's sport was played
They were given plenty for the price that they paid
This fairytale had no fire breathing dragon to slay
Just a princess who fought to survive each day
At times the princess dreamed of seeing the king's wife
But his wife lived in her own world filled with strife
The princess plodded along on the path set before her
No other existence to her did occur
The others who lived in this kingdom filled with woe
Walked through the land as though the secrets they did not know
They couldn't be expected to look to close and see
The kind of evil acts the king put forth in his decree
The princess dreamed of the day that it would all end
But there was no prince charming for anyone to send
The princess was left with a heart full of unshed tears

A soul that still carries scars and many unfaced fears
For many long years this fairy tale remained to anyone untold
Of a long ago princess who by a king was once sold

Terror in the Night

Some people look forward to the time of sleep and dreams
There are others who know it brings unheard screams
The end of every day brought me to terror in the night
The announcement of bedtime caused me extreme fright
I never knew if he would come carrying a belt
The physical beating would certainly leave at least one welt
Sometimes I would pray really hard that I would get beat
That seemed better than his new friends I might have to meet
Sometimes I would be able to guess once I saw his face
Sometimes there were not any feelings there, not even a trace
Mostly I was left to just wait until he made a move and see
I knew when he was finally done for the night and I would be free
The terror would start with the first step on the stair
I would count to fourteen and know he would soon be there
Oh please let him just hurry and have it be done
I had no choice, there was no chance to run
When I would hear him start up the stairs
I would begin silently to weep and utter my prayers
Please Jesus please tonight just stay right here by my side
Please do not let him see where it is that I hide
The story unfolded the same every single night
But I learned very early it was no use to fight
I always tried to believe it wouldn't happen again

But I knew to him I was just an animal in a pen
Some people can face their nights worry free
But it is not the same for someone like me
There are still many times I feel the terror of the night
I fear that forever it will be my life's soul plight

Daddy's Little Girl

I longed to be his special one
He said we would have so much fun
He didn't speak of any sacrifice
I did not understand there would be a price
I did not get willingly into his bed
I was innocent, easily led
I had no idea of the cost
It led me to a place of the lost
How will I ever again be found
Now in unseen chains forever bound
Wandering lost afloat in unbearable pain
Still daddy's love I tried so hard to gain
I could only watch from a place above
Trying to figure out how this was love
I just wanted a sweet kiss and hug
I wanted to feel all safe and snug
I wanted to be the special one
He promised me we would have fun
Now today I am forced to count the price
I now understand I was the sacrifice
I never did become the apple of daddy's eye
I swore I would try to the day that I die
I want to be someone special some day

But I am not sure I will ever be able to find a way

DON'T FEEL

Don't feel, won't feel, there is a cost
When they talk my voice is lost
Don't cry, don't let them see you
You don't want your weakness to be a clue
They prod, they want me to speak
They want to know I am truly weak
I finally beg and cry for mercy
But that brings out a different fee
Don't feel, can't feel, can't pay the price
These men who collect are not very nice
What things they want me to do
They know I must respond to the cue
Don't feel. Won't feel. Can't show my heart
That will just give them a place to start
Can I find inside me the way to hate
Or do I silently give into my fate
Don't feel, can't feel, I must learn how
That is still my belief even now
Don't feel, can't feel, can't let them see
Can't let them find inside the real me

The Wooden Doll

Can you see the wooden doll there on the bed
She has no face upon her small little head
She does not feel, she has no heart
She does not have a choice in this part
The men have no clue that she does not live
They only care what she has to give
I watch from somewhere far away
I have decided I don't want to play
The wooden doll makes me very sad
She is just a prop for men who are bad
It seems the only way to survive
Is to pretend that I am no longer alive
The wooden doll has no face
I cannot let her have that place
To give her a heart and let her feel
Would say that I agree with this deal
Those men who came to frolic and play
Were not interested in what she would say
They just expected her the secrets to keep
They never knew when she all alone would weep
Today I still have a price that I pay
I sometimes do not know what to say
I want to yell to scream and to cry

Sometimes I cannot even tell you why
I know I need someone who can help me through
To see all these things from a different view
My Father in Heaven has given me that way
Now I must learn to trust and walk each day

What money bought

My daddy told me to go with the men and be nice
What little girls are made of, sugar and spice
Do whatever they ask of you without any fight
It may seem wrong but I am saying it is right
I will get the report when they bring you back
I better not hear that your performance did lack
The men will tell you just what it is they seek
Your job is to give them what they want not to act meek
The negotiations were done and the price had been set
For daddy's little girl, whom the men had not met
It was all about each man and his idea of fun
And a beautiful little girl who knew no where to run
Money was exchanged and the little girl's body lent
Each man thought his money was very well spent
She never argued or fussed for she did not dare
She would just lie there for them with her little body bare
Many times the little girl watched as the money was traded
Sometimes even while she still lay naked there on the bed
Daddy says for a very good price she was sold
He had to make his money before she was too old
Daddy said each man gave him a good price
There was nothing of her he would not sacrifice
She never knew exactly for what price she was bought

She just dreamed of a day that he would be caught
It mattered to none of them when she cried stop please
For the men had already paid daddy the requested fees
The little girl learned just what their money could buy
But she has never found the answers when she cries out why

THE BOX

The punishment always seemed severe for the crime
You never knew when it would be required to do the time
There was always a prayer and a small hope
That it would be one way to survive and cope
But when the men would laugh and say, "The Box"
And I would hear them as they jingled the locks
I cannot express in words the great fear
When I heard them say, "The Box" is now here
It was no joke, "The Box" was very real
They knew exactly how their threat made me feel
They wanted me to believe they held all the power
The men wanted to see me shrink and cower
I knew when it was time it would be easier not to fight
The box in the ground was my most feared plight
Instead of the box, I would beg to be beat
Even if they did it while I hung from my feet
They laughed and they jeered at my feeble request
I never found from their evil ways any way to rest
And so I found myself once more in, "The Box"
I laid there silently weeping as they placed the locks
My spirit, soul, and body were by evil bound
It was not in my best interest to utter one sound
These men must have known I was defective from my birth

33

They made me believe I did not come from heaven to earth
I laid in that box and I laid so very, very still
As I listened to the men talk of their great thrill
It made me believe as a little girl they had all the control
They used many ways to achieve that special goal
There was still always one last prayer of hope
That somehow, someway with this I could cope

Giants

There are giants in this land
One finger as big as my hand
It is true they live in my mind
But they are of the scariest kind
The first of the giants is called fear
He always stays so very near
He has been there since I was just small
He met me as a child in the closet hall
Abandonment and rejection are two other
They were sent by my father and my mother
These two have been there since I was born
They have always made me feel alone and forlorn
The biggest giant of them is called shame
He maybe the hardest one of all to tame
If the work is slow it can be done
And then on more battle will be won
Still other giants occupy the land
They cannot be numbered on just one hand
The giants live in both my mind and soul
And when they are conquered I will be whole
The giants are known by many a name
But what they have done to me is all the same
It will take more than me to force them to go

BARBARA MCDANNELL

Now that their existence we all know

THE LIONS DEN

I spent many days in the midst of the lions den
My enemies were not animals but they were men
They looked at me as such easy prey
My crying and begging could not the men sway
The men paid no heed to my various pleas
I was just expected to give in and their wishes appease
The terror still resides deep within my heart
A lifetime of terror to me it did forever impart
I wish I pray to leave it all behind
But many days to the darkness I am still confined
Part of my mind and heart are locked in a cage
Always lurking near are fear, confusion, and rage
Somewhere, somehow there must be a magical key
Perhaps some kind of potion to clean up the debris
My enemies may not still be physically near
But that does not mean the effects will disappear
Buried deep in my innermost spirit and mind
It all seems to be forever in my core entwined
My enemies may have appeared just ordinary men
But I am sure they were closer to the animals in the den
My future has always seemed plagued by the dark
I pray every day for some light to come just a small little spark
There are many times I lose sight of the hope

And need those around me to remind me I know how to cope
I will never go back into the lions den
Not with those animals who called themselves men

IN MY DREAMS

Sometimes at night when I drift into the place of dreams
There are stories played out there and they have various themes
Sometimes I see myself as a playful little girl running
My freedom and lack of care is absolutely stunning
Some of my dreams are of being someone of great acclaim
Achieving fortune, recognition, and lots of worldly fame
Sometimes I dream of being in heaven where children are safe
Where I am greatly loved and not an unkempt little waif
The dreams change and become what life is really
A place where I was not allowed to run and roam freely
My darkest nights are where I must face my fear
Those are the dreams where my dad will suddenly appear
I wake up and do not remember where it is I am
Still feeling a lifetime ago when I was a sacrificial lamb
I must quiet my breathing and my heart rate
Realize that I cannot allow the feelings of hate
I am all grown up now and need not be afraid
These are the days for which I longingly prayed
Dreams are just dreams and are not reality
I have survived without becoming a fatality
It is true that some dreams still show what's locked inside
Dreams that show those things I still try to hide
For now, is that when I am fully awake

I will find ways to stop all of my heartache
Sometimes at night when I drift off to sleep
I wish for a safe world to hold onto and keep

The Penny Bracelet

Oh how I dreamed of the penny bracelet
Maybe a necklace to finish out the set
Each penny found as I scanned the piles
All of them traveled over so many miles
I polished and shined each one of them
Each one I considered a special gem
Pennies from the year of my earthly start
Collected and cherished with all of my heart
I dreamed of how they would shine
They would be so special when they were all mine
How sad it was when the bracelet finally came
It just was not at all the same
It came as a pay off for acts done in the dark
Acts that caused my soul to bear an eternal mark
He thought he would give it with gratitude
However that was not the receiver's mood
It only made deeper the hurt and the pain
She saw it and it drove her deeper towards being insane
The dream of the bracelet was forever shattered
A physical body that was bruised and battered
She never wore that bracelet not even one time
It represented her souls dirt and grime
That is when I knew for the first time dreams did not matter

Not to a little girl's soul that was shattered

The Closet Child

The closet was nothing but empty space
Except for a child who needed a hiding place
Behind all the old coats hung on a rack
The closet child lay alone shivering in the back
Every night she would pray for a wall
To hide her away in the closet in the hall
How she would pray for a quick sudden death
She hoped that she would take her last breath
It never failed each night he would come
His breath smelled of whiskey or was it rum
She already knew the games he wanted to play
It was always the same played, only his way
She could hear his very first step on the stair
She knew he would find her again hiding there
She would hear him walk to the closet door
Then he would take her for himself once more
Then came a night when she drew on her fear
She carefully planned what to do when he got near
It was the first time the child decided to fight
She used all her strength to hit kick and bite
He was so quick when he struck the child
He whispered he loved for her to be wild
"GO Ahead," he screamed as he again slapped her

The fight from you just makes it seem better
The child stopped and she grew very still
She had just lost all of her will
The closet child was not given a choice
The closet child was not given a voice
The child knew there was nowhere safe
The closet child was just a poor little waif
Every night the closet child went back
Behind all the coats hung on the rack
Each night she would return to her hiding place
Her soul and her closet were both empty space
The child was nothing but his personal whore
Pain and sorrow ran deep to her very core

DADDY'S BIG HANDS

His hands seemed so huge to a girl of my size
I had not yet learned those hands to despise
I yearned for him to use those hands to hold me
Or at least to lift me up and set me on his knee
Then as I sat on his knee he would tell me of his love
Share stories and teach me about the Father I have above
I wanted him to take hold of my tiny little hand
Take me for a long walk or play in the sand
I try hard but am unable to remember any of those times
What I do remember are the hands that did unthinkable crimes
Most of my life those hands caused me fear and terror
A dad and his love all seemingly just a little girls error
The times that he touched me with those big hands
Were not what I wanted, desired or had planned
He used his hands for touching his daughter in pure lust
It brought me to a lifetime of living with my own disgust
When daddy died and I stood at his casket side
His hands were what stood out as I stood and cried
They seemed extra large and as if made of something like wax
As though even in death they would be responsible for his heinous
acts
Today I still long for his big strong hands to embrace me
I still wrongly believe that it will somehow help me to see

That the things those hands and that man did with them
Have not ever truly determined in life who I am
I still need someone with earthly hands that are unstained
To make sense of a lifetime of his acts unexplained
His hands seemed so huge to a girl of my size
Who knows now why she learned those hands to despise

Tale of Two Frogs

The tale of two frogs has been told
It is new to me though very old
Two frogs who each had a different view
This tale provided a valuable clue
Two little frogs fell into a bucket of cream
Neither one of them had a viable scheme
So both little frogs began to swim
Oh but the outlook appeared to be grim
One little frog swam until he was very tired
A new plan to find he was not inspired
The other little frog swam very hard
Being so very tired he paid no regard
The first little frog just quit and he drowned
The second little frog kept swimming around
The second little frog began to churn butter
He didn't waste time in that cream to mutter
Once the work of cream to butter was done
Clear to see which frog was the determined one
One frog died, he gave up the fight
The other persevered and found a life bright
My cream is made of pain, shame and grief
At times giving up has been my true belief
Now I know the answer is continue and move through

And churn my cream into something so new
The question now lingers for me in my life
Will I be the drowned frog beaten by strife
Or will I keep swimming until I churn butter
Continue to move forward or lay down and sputter

Voices in the Night

Ssshh!! Listen very carefully
Can you hear them too
Or do they merely echo in my mind
A mix of past and present pain
Ssshhh!! They are a little muffled
But if you are patient a moment
You can hear the anguished cries
Of a spirit as it dies
Ssshhh!! That is a small child's voice
Her screams are mingled with tears
Of fear and shame and an empty heart
And of desperately wanting to be loved
Ssshh!! The voice in now that of a woman
Mixed with pain and years of shame
Feelings so overwhelming and unexpected
With no where to let them go
Ssshhh!! You can hear them too
The child and the woman now one
Please just stay, don't hurry off
Let them know you hear them cry
Ssshhh!!! They are very real
Are you strong enough for them
Let them know you are here

BARBARA MCDANNELL

Reach out and hold their hands

Samuel

You were loved from the moment I heard
Your mama texted I'm "pregnant" a magical word
For years we talked, plotted and had made a plan
In those first moments through my mind it all ran
I pondered how your mother must be feeling joy
She did not know she was carrying a little baby boy
A baby that was created from the Father's pure love
Rejoicing for your life with the angels high above
Your mother's true heart was not really on display
The price to hold you she was not willing to pay
To see your life spared inside my heart burned
Answer to prayer and decisions changed is what I yearned
Your life way to suddenly taken before your physical birth
But still you held a precious heavenly worth
Samuel Joseph, for your life I still daily weep
The sorrow comes from a place so very deep
The heavenly angels for now assigned to your care
Jesus helps me with the grief for you I alone bare
This earth was not meant to be your permanent home
You were destined among the angels to play and roam
You must now know why you were not left her to live
The precious lessons that you were meant to give
And so carried in my heart with love you will always be

The impact of your life someday in full I will be able to see

Where are the children

Where are the children
The plan was for ten
The children who would be mine
Coming one at a time down the line
A mother my only goal from the start
Each dreamed of child created in my heart
Each one already given their own special name
Each one to grow and develop their own fame
Who would have ever guessed there would be none
Not one little daughter, not one precious son
No children of mine to love and to hold
None in my image to teach, love and mold
Where are my ten children
I am left broken and barren
Ten children meant to be mine
None of them here to form the line
This is a wound in my soul so deep
It causes me alone at night to weep
Seemingly nothing here to fill that space
Who is there that understands this my place
Where are my children numbering ten
Are they left waiting for a mother in heaven
Where are the little ones meant to be mine

Can't someone please tell me or give a sign

The Naming

A child was born and was given a name
It was changed, it did not stay the same
The mother chose one and did not confer
The father came and picked a new one for her
The child grew and was only known by one
A name the child wished she could shun
As she grew she shortened the name some
When called by the full name she would go numb
Only one man called her by the name she was given
A man still in her life who has never been forgiven
The child cannot even choke out the name
Merely hearing it can make her recall all the shame
The child calls herself many other things
To any other name she gladly longingly clings
Those who know and understand her pain
Know that for a new name she would gladly campaign
All her life she has hated the name and it's sound
But yet in her life a new name has not been found
That child that name that time maybe better forgot
It all still leaves her stomach and throat in a knot
Will she one day be proud to claim her given name
Only when she can say it without feeling all of the shame

My Girls

Contessa, you are the baby I could never hold
My love and longing for you will never grow cold
You grew for a short time inside of me
Your life here on earth never came to be
You have been revealed in my true heart
While I remain on earth we will be apart
Once your existence was buried deep in my grief
Your life was stolen from me by an evil thief
God planned your days although they were few
Only He knew just when you were really due
You spend every day in a land with angels
Listening to them and Jesus and sweet stories they tell
Temperance, you were my second baby girl born
But your very existence forever into secrecy sworn
Those evil men allowed you at least one breath
But then swiftly with their hands caused your death
You were placed in my arms for a very short time
Then snatched away, again without any reason or rhyme
My heart and my arms for you today still ache
But your memory no man can ever from me take
Now your sister and you both live on eternally
Some day we will all be together again as a family

My personal Psalm

As the life sustaining roots
Of every green plant He created
Reach into the deepest soil
To fulfill its need for life giving nutrients
So my spirit which You also created
Longs to reach deeply into Your scriptures
Where I can find life sustaining words
To feed my spirit
As the sun rises every morning
In natural splendor and glory
So my spirit desires to rise
In praise to You who reigns
As King of Kings and Lord of Lords
As the drought stricken lands
Desperately need the refreshing rain
So I need the refreshment of Your love
And the knowledge of Your presence
And Your unfathomable love for me

From a Tangle of Weeds

In a field filled with thorns and weed
Heavenly Father planted a single flower seed
Tenderly it was placed by the Father's hand
Only He knew just what was planned
Each day the weeds grew thick and tall
Building a seemingly unbreakable wall
The Father saw it had water and light
So it would grow in both stature and might
Somehow that little seed found life
Even though tangled in weeds of strife
Finally among the weeds a flower stood
Where no one ever thought that there could
This lesson I will remember all my days
Heavenly Father has only good ways
In the midst of my life's tangled weeds
I was once planted as a tiny seed
He tenderly placed me here by His hand
He's always known just what He had planned
He keeps me carefully always in His sight
He makes sure I am led to the light
So among life's weeds someday a flower I'll stand
Tenderly placed by my Father's gentle hand

www.ingramcontent.com/pod-product-compliance
Lightning Source LLC
Chambersburg PA
CBHW031425160726
47993CB00003B/1401